DON'T FEED THE DUCKS!

DON'T FEED THE DUCKS!

Overcoming Unhealthy Helping in Your Life
& Relationships

by John Raven

Bird House
PUBLISHING

Don't Feed the Ducks!

Overcoming Unhealthy Helping in your Life & Relationships

ISBN-13: 978-1495376993
ISBN-10: 1495376990

Copyright © 2014

Author: John Raven, MS

Editor: Edward Morris • edwardrmorrisjr.blogspot.com

Cover and Interior Design: TKDeal Art • www.tkdealart.com

A Bird House Publishing booklet.

Contents

Acknowledgements

F or over the last fifteen years, I have had the desire to share the ideas, theories, practice, personal anecdotes and stories that went into this book. And as I wrote it, it was deeply important to me to share what I believe in as truthful a manner as possible.

So when it came time to pen this portion, I struggled with a bit of a paradox. How could I acknowledge that the help and support of so many people went into the completion of this book, a book in part about learning why self-reliance is so important? In my mind, there was a sense of hypocrisy in the appearance that my message applies to you, but somehow I am exempt from abiding by it. That did not meet my desire for integrity, meaning, and purpose.

Of course, quite ironically, through the continued support of peers, family and friends, I was able to move past this roadblock. I was reminded that living with this dissonance is just a part of the package deal of life.

In the war against codependence, poor social boundaries, unhealthy helping, and all the other painful inner demons that lead to a loss of self, the most powerful weapon in the arsenal of dysfunction is the seductive idea that imperfection is unacceptable.

"Your book is fine, John. Stop feeding your ducks," said a friend with a wry, supportive grin. I took this all in with a deep breath and a smile. So I would like to thank those that helped me on my path, a path that accepts the

1

many grey areas and paradoxes that are inherent to humanity, and to use forgiveness in abundance to live a life truly worth living. I would also like to thank my father. For, despite my many early-adulthood lamentations, I am actually quite grateful for the less-than-voluntary writing sessions he gave me.

Though difficult as it may have been for me to see at age twelve, the summer days spent writing and revising paragraphs (despite my heavily-verbalized desire to instead watch cartoons or some other equally slothful pre-teen endeavor) have been immeasurably helpful in my life. No doubt, his guidance helped shape my eventual zest for the written word and is likely much of the reason these words have been brought to the page.

Foreword

This is a book for those who want to help others, to teach them to be able to do so, in any instance, and not be swallowed up by it. Often I'm tasked with the difficult job as a therapist, which is to manage the answers to questions people come to me with, such as "How can I fix him/her/them/it?", instead of being asked the more pertinent question: "Is my heart in the right place?"

This rarely-questioned belief, that the imperative to help is not only necessary but presumed to be coming from a selfless, healthy place is as unfortunate as it is often. We as helpers, healers, parents, friends, lovers, partners...humans, need to know that compassion and self-preservation are not mutually exclusive. There needs to be room for both. In this book, there are tools presented for both helping more effectively and asserting your own desires.

I often ask new counseling patients point-blank, "What are you here for? How do you think things are going?" And I will do you no disservice by doing anything different herein. This is done with the intention of holding up a mirror to see what is truly going on so that you can make the rest of the judgment for yourself. As much as I would love for it to be true, I don't have all the answers.

I hope you'll find this book a powerful set of tools and truths which, when used properly, can yield amazingly positive results in your life. If you're anything like the many wonderful people I have helped in the past, you will find much of the ideas and strategies presented here to be a welcome relief. And if something doesn't work for you, that's okay too! Similar to the concept put forth in Alcoholics Anonymous, I invite you to 'take what you want, and leave the rest.'

When I began writing this book, my goal was to help people I couldn't reach individually by creating a compendium of all the tidbits of knowledge and wisdom I've learned from years of counseling practice. I wanted to make that knowledge available to anyone who has a family member suffering from addiction or severe mental health problems.

As I began, I discovered that the work quickly transformed from a rough collection of advice and very specific solutions for specific people to a radical change-in-life philosophy for anyone. It covers a gamut of things, from how to approach loaning a friend ten dollars to fundamentally altering your way of being in the world.

The only agenda I have is to help you live a more satisfying existence. I use imagery and metaphor throughout the book to help you understand the concepts and apply them to your life.

This book will provide less of a step-by-step guide for how to live your life than a framework for making better choices. It can serve as a guide to help you make short-term, immediate decisions, and even guide you toward resolution of lifelong, systemic issues.

Rather than teach you what not to do, this book will suggest what *to* do, which is to utilize an intentional and purposeful analysis of your thoughts and beliefs to propel you into a new way to look at the world.

I promise not to sell you the written form of snake-oil. I have no magic cure. To the best of my knowledge, there isn't one. All I can offer you is the simple idea that exploring the depths of your potential boldly can bring about a change you may never have thought possible.

Odd though it may sound, your greatest asset will be your willingness to acknowledge that things aren't working very well the way you have been doing them, and that you are open to trying something new. I merely offer the tools, and the promise that I have seen this work in the lives of hundreds of individuals I have worked with.

Please understand, too, that half-hearted gestures are pretty useless. If you're not prepared to go all the way with it, neither this nor any other approach is likely to bring you the changes you seek.

So let's finish the job together. You will have plateaus along the way, but I encourage you not to settle for simple relief. Hold out instead for a more total life change, and be confident that you can and will get there.

Often, people solicit the help of others to commiserate with them, only to gain short-term relief, rather than real, lasting change. If a friend asked you to patch a tire that would only get them another ten miles when you could simply replace it, wouldn't it make more sense to replace it?

If I were to help clean up your life just enough to keep you going until the next crisis, this would likewise be of no true help to you. I have loftier goals in mind, and faith that you can achieve them.

Sometimes there are moments when we have perfect clarity about our problems. We see everything and say, "My God, this is what I have been doing to myself!" My hope is to inspire you to have one of those moments, when you realize the violent consequences that repeated irrational thinking have had on your soul.

I want to inspire one of those moments when you really feel the raw emotion and energy around seeing the true nature of your decisions, but before you retreat into shame, fear, and guilt, I hope to inject a cure that will remain active long enough to dislodge the poison.

I won't soften the blow for you. If you are willing to do the fearless work necessary, you will see positive change in your life. It is presented in a frank and scrupulously honest manner, in the hope that you will become practiced and successful at self-exploration and healthy boundary setting.

So, let's get quacking!

Amy's Story

"Kindness can go too high,
even in Heaven
as a bird carrying a fish out of water
to give it air."

WITTER BYNNER
(American poet, 1881-1968)

my was exhausted. Hugging the oversized pillow on
my office couch, she stared blankly at the wall. Her
husband, a successful businessman, was teetering on the
edge of an alcoholic breakdown. Overwhelmed by the
crippling fear that the life she'd created for herself was
falling apart, she came to me for help.

Since the earliest days of their marriage, she quietly took
care of him. This included cleaning up his beer cans before
the children woke up, turning off the television, and
tucking him in on the couch when he passed out, then
making sure he woke up in time for work.

In addition, Amy felt that she was under pressure to
ensure that the lives of her two children were 'perfect.' This
kept her obsessing over every detail of their lives to make
sure everything was taken care of.

Amy self-reported feeling happy much of the time. Yet
she also felt resentful about her obligations to participate
in the PTA, coach her daughter's soccer team, and attend

church club events, *et cetera, ad nauseam.* Her life was full, yet she was miserable, living in nearly-constant terror that she wasn't doing enough. Amy felt that her life wasn't her own.

I asked Amy where the emotional Safe Place was in her own life and daily routine. Her face brightened. An impish smile appeared.

"Well, I know I'm not supposed to do this, but we have this little duck pond near my house. I love to go down to the pond and feed the ducks." As soon as she mentioned this, I saw a little flash of disappointment in her eyes. I called her attention to what I had just observed, and I asked her tell me what she was feeling.

After a moment's pause, she said that as soon as she mentioned the ducks, she felt an overwhelming sense of guilt, because she doesn't go feed them enough, and they have come to be so dependent on her. She felt shame, too, for feeding them even though there was a very prominent sign at the pond which read DON'T FEED THE DUCKS.

Amy told me that she brought them two or three bags of bread at a time, saved leftover bread her kids and husband didn't eat at meals, and even bought feed sometimes, yet continued to feel that this was never enough.

After she was out of bread, the ducks would crowd around her, begging for more. And she would actually verbally apologize to them. At this point in her story, Amy burst into tears.

Like many I have had the opportunity to counsel, Amy

struggled much of her life with an intrusive and exaggerated sense of responsibility. This sense in her was so strong that intentionally or not, it kept her from meeting her own needs. Amy was among those whom Melody Beattie, author of *Codependent No More,* memorably describes as "responsible for the entire world, yet refuse to take responsibility for leading their own lives."

Amy came to me hoping for a solution to all her problems. She was surprised (and probably a little annoyed) to find out that part of my counseling philosophy is that I can't solve problems for anyone. All I can do is to help them remove the mental blocks that hold them back by asking for some sincere, and sometimes painful, self-examination.

Mental blocks have physical manifestations, and when that self-examination becomes less painful, the overall physical and spiritual health the person show a clear corollary with the calluses they've built up by confronting the issue.

In my best estimation, Amy intrinsically knew what her problem was, but due to habit, temperament, upbringing, and a host of other obstacles, she was unable to find a satisfying resolution. The closer she got to the root of her problem, the more she drew away from the solution.

This is common for so many people who have difficulties with "feeding the ducks." People get stuck in a loop that demands that they continue to do the one thing that keeps them miserable. For Amy, as for many others, the desire to be defined by the energy she poured into the needs of others eclipsed her own need for personal mental health. The more she looked to others to fulfill her own sense of self, the less she felt that sense. Yet, she was simultaneously even less inclined to do anything to fulfill that need within herself. Amy felt that she needed her husband and children to continually give her a sense of identity.

Once she was able to look beneath the pain, frustration, and anxiety, and past her stubborn desire to have the heavens magically open up and give her a sense of purpose, Amy found a new hope. Oddly enough, one of Amy's strengths was that she was willing to admit her misery. It drove her to take those first tentative steps forward and finally to scream, "ENOUGH!" When she was able to do so, she finally recognized just how miserable she actually was.

I noticed that the more she was able to look at her own beliefs and question them, the easier change became for her. One of the first things Amy realized was that the more tightly she grasped her vision of perfection, the more it slipped away. She was able to understand the situation she was placing herself in, and resolved to start changing her behavior.

I've often heard the axiom, "Change the reaction and you change the behavior. Amy was well on her way toward understanding the very concept that I myself had stumbled upon.

She'd begun to unlock the rush of relief that comes with casting aside the anxiety and burden of expectations, and obtaining resolution through purposeful awareness of her own beliefs. It wasn't until she started focusing on her needs, her happiness, and ways she could make her life work for her (rather than constantly having to work for others) that she began to find a sense of fulfillment.

Along the way, I'm also happy to report that she also stopped feeding the ducks at the duck pond.

Your Life, Your Pond

Nine times out of ten, when a client comes to me trying to learn how to change someone else, changing that other person is the last thing that needs to happen. Often the change must occur within the petitioner to be concurrent with what's needed to fix the actual problem. Not always, but in most cases.

This may sound mystifying. It should.

Our inborn ego defenses aren't designed to have that level of introspection come naturally or easily. As amazing as it would be for us to take on the *responsibility* of changing our environment, more often than not, we see it as *blame*, and our ego-state is hard-wired to reject blame.

I imagine if I started out any clinical relationship by saying, "Listen, it's about you, not anything or anybody else. The problem is with you. Change yourself and you'll be fine," the conversation wouldn't go well from there. Not only is it hubris to think that would work (after all, if it's really that simple, would they even need to solicit my services?), but also, my brash bedside manner would find me with an empty client list very quickly.

I have instead found that in addition to offering empathy, understanding and support, that metaphors are incredibly powerful tools to help us move past our own defenses and come to resolution. I like to think of metaphors as fun, creative little backdoors to help us hack our way into the brain.

One of my favorite genres, Science Fiction, uses metaphor quite brilliantly. I can think of no better example of this clever phenomenon than the now infamous Star Trek episode "Let That Be Your Last Battlefield."

In the episode, two races of humanoids living on the same planet share a burning hatred for each other. Biologically their only difference is that one race is half white on the right side, half black on the left, and the other the opposite, half white on the left side, half black on the right.

This minute variance is seemingly in-distinguishable to the confused crew of the Enterprise, yet is enough of an impetus for brutal war and violence between the races. This is shown well when Bele, one of the main protagonists of the episode, meets with Kirk and Spock.

It is revealed that Bele believes his coloration to be superior to his counterpart Lokai's — "I am black on the *right* side. Lokai is *white* on the right side. All of his people are white on the right side" — even though Kirk and crew sees no difference in the two and vehemently disagree with his convictions of racial superiority.

The juxtaposition of this absurdity was an excellent tool at the time (the late 1960's) for Americans to have a conversation about the painful topic of racism in our communities, and to move past the often blinding handicap of our own subjective experience. It's hard to see how absurd judgment based on skin color is when it is an ingrained part of society, yet so simple to see the extent of the illogic when viewed through the lens of theoretical space men in the sky.

Similarly, breaking down the ego-defenses that keep us from realizing problematic thinking can be had in this way when talking about unhealthy helping.

Imagine for a moment that the world you live in is a park surrounding a pond. Nothing exists outside this imaginary ten-acre pond area. There's a walking path around the pond, some grass, a few nice trees—and nothing else.

Each item in your life might represent part of the park. The bench you sit at could perhaps be your home, providing comfort and a place to call your own. Perhaps the trees and the walkways surrounding the pond represent good memories, or the path you've created for your life. There are people who come and go from your pond, and animals which could represent people as well.

The songbirds in the trees sing the rousing songs sung by those who champion your life, your cheerleaders to success. The squirrels might represent acquaintances along the way that watch curiously from afar, or sometimes ignore you altogether.

In this framework, the ducks represent people who are emotionally or otherwise needy. They swoop, circle a few times, and then glide in to touch down in your pond.

Hungry, looking for respite and a bit of attention, they seek the easiest solution to their problems. Seeing the familiar silhouette of an all-too-eager person with a bag of feed or bread, they furiously scurry toward you to gobble up what you have to offer.

You feed them bread, bits of grain, maybe popcorn. All that uneaten bread and seed falls to the bottom of the pond. It helps feed the non-native invasive fish, such as carp and suckerfish. It kills the natural underwater breeding grounds for the native species to reproduce in. This, too, is the metaphorical fallout that helping these ducks has on your pond, on your life.

Most food that people give to ducks is not nutritionally sound for them. It fills their bellies, but doesn't give them the energy they need to survive, and can cause digestive obstructions of several different varieties. In addition, it trains them to get food from humans, instead of scuffling and surviving on their own, which ultimately is best for them. They become bolder and more aggressive around humans, which put them at risk for transmitting or receiving diseases.

They also tend to start nipping when they don't get what they want, putting them at further risk for needing to be euthanized for becoming a public nuisance. Possibly worse of all, feeling that they have a comfortable safe haven with an abundance of food, they will delay their journey south before the winter, putting them at risk of starving on their way.

Now imagine translating the concepts of this metaphorical world into your current world. This could relate to any number of situations. Are there any "ducks" that you feed?

Perhaps you have a child that often finds themselves on the hard-luck side of finances. Do you feel compelled to bail them out? Do you perhaps have a friend that you feel often obligated to rescue from problem relationships? Is there an addict or alcoholic in your life who you have been "feeding?"

There are multitudes of ways this can become a problem. Is "feeding" them actually harming their progress? By doing so, are you actually preventing them from learning a lesson they need in order to grow and move on?

Are there situations in your life in which you feel so compelled, through sadness or an overdeveloped sense of compassion, to feed those ducks, even though you know it's wrong?

Do you, perhaps, through feeding those ducks, develop a false sense of authority or power? Do you find yourself surrounded by needy ducks that you try to help, only to find yourself frustrated and overwhelmed by sheer size of the flock? Do you find yourself then resentful of them because you're so giving, only to not have the favor returned when you need help.

Throughout this book, this metaphor characterizes how and why we do what we often do in relationships, and ways in which this can become problematic. My hope is that this will be a useful image which you can quickly draw from to guide your decision-making. It's a great way to check in with your life and relationships and how you're living them.

I use this metaphor to help clients in a counseling setting, but also I use it often myself as a mantra when I'm struggling with desires to rescue my the ducks in my life; my clients, peers, or friends. Perhaps I am feeling compelled to rescue someone from a difficult emotion I pause and think with a smile, "Don't feed the ducks, John!"

Defining Some Terms

Let's define some terms I'll be using throughout this book. I will later refer to them as parts of a whole system, so it is important to understand some new language should you decide to adopt the change I propose in this book. My hope is that you to begin developing a new culture and identity through language. Changing the way you talk can have a significant effect on how you act. Psychologists call this a *paradigm shift*.

For example, saying "I feel angry" instead of saying "I feel like I'm angry" can actually affect how you identify with your emotions (besides it being quite impossible to feel "like" something, but I'll save that for another time).

Paradigm shift—This is a radical and total change in perspective. It's one of those wonderful moments where a light bulb switches on in your brain and you see amazing and new ways to fix a problem that you never imagined before.

A paradigm shift usually involves the difficulty one faces when approaching a problem with a faulty set of beliefs and then trying to fix that problem within the confines of those faulty beliefs.

A perfect example is the Chinese finger-trap, the cylindrical gag toy made of woven bamboo, just large enough to fit the size of most fingers. The natural tendency, once you insert a finger in each end, is to pull to get your fingers out. You find, however, that your fingers have immediately become trapped.

The harder you pull, the tighter the finger-trap becomes. You have to relax your fingers and push inward instead of pulling outwards, to loosen up the woven bamboo enough to twist your fingers out. The faulty premise that keeps most stuck in the trap is that "I must not be pulling hard enough," or perhaps, "Pulling away from this trap is the only way to get out."

A paradigm shift involves thinking creatively about doing something outside that logical box to try and solve the problem. A paradigm shift often is accompanied by that euphoric "A-ha!" in which you see something from a completely new perspective.

Another way of saying that a shift in your paradigm, or point of view, is present is that you conceptually are 'learning by unlearning'. That is to say, that you have to go back to beliefs that you assumed were fact (for example, starting with the fundamentally flawed belief that the only way out of the finger trap is by pulling) and you input new factual information (for example, saying "well pulling my fingers out is one way, but not the *only* way to get out).

Another illustration of this idea is known as the duck–rabbit optical illusion (figure on the following page). When viewed from one angle, the above image appears to be a' duck (again, fitting the theme well). When looking at it from another angle, it can be seen as a rabbit. Shifting your paradigm causes you to see the same information in a different way.

The problem with a paradigm is that once we get stuck with a belief (such as: "That's a picture of a duck and that's all I can see is a duck, there's nothing more there,"), it's quite difficult to see things a different way. The premises you initially believe about your situation may not be true, and I encourage you to examine them from many viewpoints.

Codependency—This may be a familiar term to anyone who has experience with alcoholism or drug counseling. You perhaps may have heard it in a variety of contexts. When I use this term, I'm not intending to try and diagnose anyone with a disorder, but merely to bring clarity to an issue they are having difficulty with.

Codependency is the compulsive desire to try and help others that can lead one to an excessive tendency towards taking care of them. Typically this is due to an unmet need within oneself. The unfortunate side effect of this excessive tendency is grave emotional distress, as the dysfunctional behavior inhibits their ability to effectively manage their life.

Unhealthy helping—Similar in style to codependency, but perhaps to a lesser degree, is unhealthy helping. This is when the help-er's efforts actually harm the help-ee. The classic example of this is a spouse calling in "sick" for a husband/wife who is hungover yet again, thinking this will help alleviate any work-related problems, but only helping to fuel the addiction.

Another example would be a mother who continually bails her daughter out by paying the overdraft fees on the daughter's checking account, thus never allowing the daughter to learn proper money management skills. This leads to the next definition.

Feedback loop—A feedback loop is traditionally an acoustic term. The most common time we see a feedback loop is when a singer is too close to a microphone and a loud squelch is heard through the speakers. The microphone then picks up this noise and feeds it back into the speakers again. The result is a loud, grating noise loop (which usually causes us, the listeners, to cover our ears in pain).

A feedback loop in this context means that one is stuck

in a pattern in which the behaviors we exhibit to try and make the situation better actually feed the outcomes that make our situation worse. Then, when we increase our efforts to make things better, the behavior is met with an equally-increasing intensity.

An example of this would be a spouse attempting to awaken their alcoholic and very hung-over spouse so that the spouse isn't late for work. Then the alcoholic spouse comes to rely on them as an alarm clock. They think "Well, I can get as drunk as I want tonight, because my husband/wife will wake me up."

Feedback loops continues to spiral out of control as the attempts to remedy the situation (more helping behavior) actually make the situation worse.

Temperament and upbringing—Upbringing refers to one's collection of experiences, while temperament refers to an individual's emotional and personality makeup. I want to avoid falling into the old 'Nature vs. Nurture' debate, but suffice it to say that temperament and upbringing have a great deal to do with how you turn out as an adult.

Upbringing is used to describe the environment you grow up in (middle class, urban/rural, Italian-American neighborhood, etc.) and the experiences you have while growing up. If one exact clone of you were dropped off in rural China; and another in Poughkeepsie, New York, the two of you, though biologically similar, would have differences in attitude and beliefs depending on who raised you, the environment you were raised in, and experiences during your child rearing.

Temperament encompasses the biologically passed-down traits that we come with as humans. It's the genetic dice-roll that we use when interacting with the world. The term temperament is used a lot to refer to the behaviors of babies, such as "Jerry has such a calm temperament. He just lies in his crib and never makes a peep."

Actor-observer bias—This is the psychological phenomenon in which humans have the tendency to ascribe 'fault' or 'blame' for situational difficulties on the outside world rather than on ourselves. For example, if you are walking along on the street and perhaps your shoe catches a crack in the sidewalk and you stumble, your brain is most likely going to assign 'blame' for the accident on the sidewalk (the external world), rather than blame yourself.

This isn't always the case, in fact, in extreme cases of problematic self-esteem and guilt people default to everything being their fault, but typically research has shown that this is the tendency of the human brain. The actor-observer bias is a very handy tool to keep depression and self-doubt at bay, but when applied too much or too often it can become problematic.

The actor-observer bias actually is the counterpart to another interesting concept called the *fundamental attribution error*, an error in which others tend to assign blame or responsibility for a person's acts on their disposition or personality rather than their situation. So in the previous example, the fundamental attribution error says that if you trip on a crack in the sidewalk, a person who saw you trip is more likely to assume that it's because you are clumsy, not because the sidewalk was at fault.

Now that we've learned some new verbiage, or perhaps reviewed some which is already familiar, we can begin to comprehend some of the ways in which an individual's upbringing and temperament can combine in such a way that they're prone to codependency or unhealthy helping.

This leads them into a feedback loop, wherein they keep feeding the ducks in their lives. Because of the actor-observer bias and other psychological concepts, a person has great difficulty realizing that the problem lies not with the world around them, but with their own interpretation of the world. It takes a paradigm shift to dislodge the thinking that causes the problem.

Some Assumptions

*"Begin challenging your own assumptions. Your
assumptions are your windows on the world. Scrub them
off every once in a while, or the light won't come in."*

ALAN ALDA

Some basic assumptions throughout this work are
necessary as well to provide foundations for us to
begin building on. Many of the concepts in this book won't
make a whole lot of sense without them.

It may be difficult to understand why I put forth the
beliefs that I do without considering these four key
concepts. The philosophical underpinnings of these
assumptions have far-reaching implications for most of this
book, so it's important to spend some time explaining
them, at least in brief.

I won't give them the justice they deserve, because entire
volumes of books have been written on each one of these
topics, but for the sake of building a framework together,
here they are.

Assumption #1: You Can't "Make Me" Feel Anything

Taking responsibility for the way you feel will allow you
to begin exerting more emotional stability in your life.

Others can influence the way we feel, but can never directly cause you to feel a certain way. It is at the crux of this distinction that change can and will happen.

This is not meant in a depressive or shaming way that faults a person for having their own emotions, but rather an opportunity for new experience. And I want that experience to be empowering for you, rather than defeating.

We often get snared by the seductive allure of being the victim, and it's time to stop. This might be a bitter pill, but let's face it: How well has that been working for you? We could argue about how it's unfair to have to give up on faulting others, or how we've been wronged, but this will get us nowhere. It's time for a change!

Later in this book, I will explain how and why this seductive game happens. My hope for you is that through enlightenment, this will help end the helplessness of blaming others for your feelings. For now, however, it is enough to lay the groundwork and at least be willing to entertain the idea that this assumption is true.

Consider Sara's case:

Sitting on my therapy couch, my client 'Sara' shouted at her daughter, "This is YOUR fault!" Her arms were crossed and her face was flushed. This was no surprise, considering she'd just walked three miles from her house to our family session. As well, Sara and her daughter got into an argument en route. In a huff, Sara got out of the car and decided to walk. Sara felt slighted, angry, and wronged. Her daughter felt confused, angry, and afraid. The two had arrived in total emotional chaos.

Because I'd already worked with this family, I had some latitude in my approach. Rather than begin what would surely be a lengthy discussion about how and why the two were arguing, I instead simply asked Sara how it felt to know she was completely powerless over her emotions. She looked at me quizzically and asked me to explain.

I described how she was essentially admitting that her daughter had the power to literally make her get out of the car and walk. The assumption that I believe Sara was stuck with was that others have control over how we think, feel and act and that is what leads to problems in relationships.

Then I asked Sara to consider that she was giving her daughter control of Sara's emotions. This enabled her to reframe her understanding. Once confronted with the only logical realization: that her feelings are independent of her daughter's actions, she was relieved to have an option beyond being stuck in her old dysfunctional patterns of thinking and behaving.

If we were to dissect the concept of someone making you feel something, you would perhaps realize how emotionally violent a concept this is. "He made me sad when he told me I didn't look good in those shorts." This is essentially conceding that someone else has the ability to control your emotions. They can make you sad, angry, mad happy, or loved—all at their whim. If one has no influence over how they feel, this will inevitably lead towards resentment, anger, and frustration. Instead, move toward an understanding that people have the ability to inspire or impact our decisions, but never cause them.

This is an important distinction, because it gives the brain the option of finding a solution to the problem, rather than giving the power to someone else. Even in the most extreme of cases, such as brainwashing, rape, and the untimely death of a loved one, you are still the owner of your emotions.

While it is true that these events can have a significantly more intense effect on emotions than, say, getting cut off in traffic, we still ultimately have the ability to choose the steps to take to begin to exert some balance over our emotions.

This concept may be confusing, because the opposite of it is so pervasive in our culture. Shifting responsibility for our emotions can have a romantic and almost seductive quality to it.

We as humans have a history of externalizing the cause of our emotions onto others. Songs such as Michael Jackson's "The Way You Make Me Feel," Frank Sinatra's "You Make Me Feel So Young," or the Aretha Franklin hit "You Make Me Feel Like a Natural Woman" exemplify this idea.

For some, this often a seemingly harmless alternative way of expressing what they mean, which is "I feel ___". But this sloppy habit can subconsciously lead to the practice of placing blame, fault, or responsibility on others for our feelings and emotions.

When we externalize the cause of blame, what can happen is we can then externalize the solution to our problems. This becomes a trap that can be a very subtle yet difficult paradigm to shift away from.

Begin instead to see how the language you choose leads to how the words you use can change how you feel. Try to actively change your words from the concept of "make me" towards saying "I feel _____."

I don't say this so you can place blame or shame upon yourself, but instead to feel empowered. While others can influence how we feel, this does not determine how we ultimately choose to feel.

Assumption #2: Likewise, I Can't "Make You" Feel Anything.

Often I ask clients to describe their experience with their spouse/significant other/friend. More often than not, what is presented to me is some form of the idea that "If he/she/they would just change X, then my life would be perfect, or at least better."

This is a similar logical pitfall that occurs with the previous assumption, which is essentially the idea that I can somehow control, rather than influence another person. I often see these two go hand-in-hand. Along with the idea that others control how a person feels usually comes the desire to be able to control another's feelings. One fundamental assumption of this book is that neither of these is the case, and that one must actively give up the practice of attempting to control the emotions of others. During my early clinical years, when presenting a client with feedback, I would preface the sentence with "I don't want to make you angry, but..." I thought it was a clever way to prime a client to avoid certain feelings and manipulate them into feeling the ones I wanted them to feel.

Luckily, I had a great supervisor who pointed this out to me. I had to admit that I had some grandiose ideas about control, myself. Followed to its logical conclusion, that sentence would be "I don't want to 'make' you angry, but I secretly believe I have the power to 'make' you something else!"

I wanted to control the outcome of how the person sitting across from me was 'supposed' to feel. The reality is, they have every right to feel any way they damned well please. My attempts to control the outcome of another's feelings were disingenuous, and ultimately self-serving.

Both my mistake of believing I had the power to manipulate the feelings of others, and the mistake of believing that "Everything would be fine in my life if he/she/it would just..." are both forms of the same fallacy. It is important to distinguish that not only can others not "make" us feel anything, but likewise we don't have that power over others' emotions.

While the temptation to believe this is enchanting, we must remember that the responsibility for their actions would inevitably come with that. Let's say I have the ability to make you feel anything—anger, for example. If you then acted out in that anger, I'd be responsible for your actions, wouldn't I?

Assumption #3: Reject The Notion That Life Isn't What You Make It.

This belief is the nefarious cousin of "making you feel" something. Somehow we believe that circumstances make us feel the way we do. The truth is that Life can't "make" you feel anything, either.

We need to understand the difference between influence and cause. Certainly the tragedies and joys of life have an impact on us. But we have the demonstrable ability to change the way we feel.

Much of human suffering, I believe, is attached to the narratives that we tell ourselves. The narrative most often, we begin each premise with is "my life is out of my control". Believing this can lead to so much suffering.

For starters, it immediately removes an entire swath of solutions to a problem right off the bat. It also gets us stuck in a feedback loop that involves the magical wish that "if only life would ____" which in turn leads us to feeling like helpless victims of life, rather than active agents of change, holding the seat of power over what they are able to do in life.

Life, unsurprisingly, doesn't turn out the way we want it, which confirms the original belief. Argh! The general idea of this assumption starts with the premise, "Life is neutral, and my attachment to a particular belief is what is causing my suffering, not the actual event itself". The neutrality of life opens up a world of possibilities.

Suddenly, the idea of "I'm saddled with student loan debt, a mortgage I can't afford, and my life is pretty much doomed," becomes "Okay, here are a bunch of obstacles between me and my goals, and I might be able to find a solution to some or all them."

The events are therefore unmarried from my feelings about them, and I can begin to construct solutions to my problems. Consider the difference between the following:

My mother is impossible!	This relationship hasn't gone the way I hoped, and I deeply desire change.
My boss has it out for me.	This employment situation isn't working the way I want and something needs to change.
The economy is screwing me.	I'm going to try my best and hope for success.
He/she/it won't do what I want.	This isn't getting me anywhere. I need a new solution; there's gotta be one out there.

Some Assumptions

I consider myself to be a *pragmatic optimist*. When pragmatics—the act of dealing with life in a practical context based manner—are combined with a hopeful, positive outlook on life, this often presents a down-on-the-ground interpretation of the old bromide "Hope for the best, and expect the worst."

Pragmatists often actively avoid getting bogged down in the search for the objective truth of a thing, but rather, choose to focus on what's practical. When I can take an event and see the neutrality of it, the decision to select a viewpoint of that event that will make life less of an exercise involving suffering, choosing the positive is a no-brainer.

For most people, thinking positively and striving to be your best seems the most practical. It brings the most happiness into life and gives us a lot more options than being pessimistic. A pragmatic optimist takes the idea that life can't make you feel anything and employs a trick toward it which can potentially make a mediocre life into a really great one: Adding massive optimism and hope.

For example, taking the idea of feeling you "have to", to look at it as "an opportunity to". I don't "have to" brush my teeth, but instead, here's a fun challenge to see how long I can keep my teeth healthy. Instead of bemoaning traffic in the morning every time you go to work, they take it as "an opportunity to practice my meditation skills", or even, "a chance to really enjoy the feeling of my car's leather seats." This is a radical shift for some people, but a necessary one. As a pragmatic optimist, I do this not because there is any objective truth to it, but quite practically, because it makes life easier. Easier said than done, right? Entire sects of people have devoted generations of their lives to prayer, meditation and practice in an attempt to overcome this human tendency to attach ourselves to our beliefs.

While this is, indeed, a concept that is very much easier said than done, we owe it to ourselves to continuously be improving our ability to detach from an outcome long enough to wisely decide how we wish to think, feel and act. (Should you find out how to do this consistently and effortlessly, please come and contact me!)

Assumption #4: Ignoring Is NOT Resolution

I could rephrase this assumption to say something to the effect of "Not Miserable is no substitute for Happy." So, perhaps, this is a two-part assumption. The first being, that it is important to become aware of how much our problems are affecting us. For many, there is a general lack of awareness of how bad things are, or have gotten.

I liken this to a fairly universal experience: having a sore throat. At first it starts off as a tickle in the throat. It inevitably becomes that unbearable hacking that leaves you almost afraid to swallow for fear of the pain.

Eventually, so beaten down by the constant discomfort, you become used to it, so much so that you may have even forgotten that life didn't used to be this way. This is often the experience with poor boundaries. We become so used to the slights, the micro-aggressions, and the tension, that it becomes normal and commonplace. It's as if the body and mind go so long without it, that you forget that there was a time in your life that you believed that relationships were supposed to be reciprocal, enjoyable and fair.

So it's important to bring some awareness to how much you are actually suffering if that is the case. Ground yourself in your experience and ask the question of whether or not you are satisfied, or simply tolerating the uncomfortable.

The second part of this assumption then, is to call into question ways in which we may be "kicking the can down the road" of our own happiness. For example, getting our spouse or child to only drink one six-pack at a time instead of three is not good enough.

Telling ourselves, "Well, at least she hasn't wrecked any cars lately!" is a moral compromise that slowly eats away at us whether we mean for it to or not. And just because things seem 'fine' now, doesn't mean that they have been resolved. Too often, change itself gets swept under the rug in an attempt to avoid conflict, or just frankly because forgetting is easier.

What I hope to convey is that you must give yourself permission to probe toward a resolution, even though every bone in your body may be telling you to stop. The previous notion challenges us to look deep into the crevices of many uncomfortable places, often places that we have intentionally swept away or kept hidden due to fear or pain, and to shine a light on them.

Shel Silverstein wrote a great children's story called THE GIVING TREE, wherein an anthropomorphized apple-tree gives up her every part in sequence to a child going through all eight stages of development. She does this out of pure unconditional love for the boy, and in the end she is a stump. She's okay with this. But not everyone has to be her. Or should.

I have heard people with decades of sobriety under their belts advance the opinion at many different kinds of Twelve-Step meetings that there is no true altruism, that everyone gets something out of what they do, even if it is only the endorphin rush behind the old proverb, "A thing done well is its own reward."

This muddies the waters a bit. We evolved to work together for the propagation of the species. Therefore, the endorphin rush from helping another is a built-in survival trait.

But, as stated, knowing that a brownie tastes good because of its chemical makeup does not diminish the experience of eating a brownie, any more than knowing that helping is selfish doesn't make it less meaningful.

Is This Me?

"Denial ain't just a river in Egypt."

MILTON BERLE

       Hi, I called in to get some information about addiction. I think my boyfriend might have a problem" Samantha sheepishly said through the phone.

I had been working at an addictions and mental health informational center for a few months when I took this call.

"I'm having a heck of a time hearing you, Samantha, I apologize," I replied. There was static on the phone, and when she spoke again her meek, quiet voice also sounded muffled.

"Well, I'm in the closet, hiding," she admitted. "My boyfriend is pretty drunk and would really be upset if he knew I was talking to you. Do you think that's a problem?"

Samantha had to go through a receptionist and two triage specialists, which meant a wait on the phone for about half an hour to get to me, a live counselor. All that time and effort to ask me some questions she probably already knew the answers to.

"Umm, well, I would say that if you feel uncomfortable in your own house, to the point that you feel you have to hide, things have gotten pretty bad. Wouldn't you say so?"

"I guess," Samantha admitted. She sighed, deeply. "How do I get him to stop?"

39

"Well, we can talk about that. And I'd also like to talk about you."

"Me," she said, puzzled. "Ohh, I'm fine, I just want to know how I can get him to stop drinking so much. I don't even want him to quit, I wouldn't ask that of him, but sometimes he gets too drunk. How do I stop that?"

The slow boil-up to this point, combined with Samantha's own lack of ability to be aware of the depth of her problem was clearly a barrier in the way of her living a satisfied, happy life. What's more, Samantha's problem wasn't just her boyfriend, but that her inability to see *her* part in the whole puzzle was just as much a problem as his drunken fits. Samantha had a long road ahead of her.

During my time at that job, I quickly discovered that I could, with almost 100% accuracy, be certain that if a person went through the trouble of getting me on the phone, I probably didn't need to assess whether there was a problem. The self-selecting nature of the clientele made sure of that. Many came to me with a similar intensity of ambivalence, dread, and lack of awareness.

While you may not be as bad off as poor Samantha, more than likely, you fall somewhere on the scale between believing that nothing is wrong, all the way to the "Please help, I'm at the end of my rope!" end of the spectrum. If you've made it to the fourth chapter, you probably have a sense that some of what I'm saying probably hit home. The good news is this: You have now fully separated yourself from the group who will live their entire lives without seeking change or asking for help because they don't believe they have a problem.

Pat yourself on the back for even reading this far. The idea that you are even willing to entertain a new way of being puts you leagues ahead of others in this respect.

It's entirely normal to ask yourself these questions, or entertain your own skepticism. It's a part of the process. But also, know that if you are reading this and what I say resonates with you even a little bit, more than likely you don't need a checklist, diagnosis, rulebook or fancy definition to tell you that this is you.

Having even said that, I know you may turn around the very next sentence and say "Yeah, this is me, but..." This paradox of ambivalence is a normal part of the process. I want to acknowledge the idea that whatever the case, I understand that some information I may present to you in these pages will bristle against some of your beliefs, and that you will likely have some degree of skepticism toward change.

The irony of this phenomenon is that this willful pattern of skepticism is what keeps people stuck in the first place. Often, when an individual can let go of whatever is holding them to that pattern (perhaps denial, fear, pride, or shame), this can help towards the path to not feeding those ducks!

I often liken this to the first time you ever dove off a diving-board as a kid. This experience is demonstrably startling and unfamiliar, and there is the tendency to get halfway out onto the board and decide that ambivalence is the safest behavior.

I see the clinician's role as slightly similar to that of the other kids waiting to use the diving-board, who will (in their own way, not mine) remove the option of deciding not to decide from the little Horatio hesitating up there on the bridge.

As human beings, we're supposed to be skeptical. It keeps us safe from the dangers of tall diving boards, but it also keeps us stuck at the top of tall diving boards paralyzed with indecision and fear. This can actually lead the mind to start convincing itself that the safest place to be is in the space of indecision. It goes something like this:

1. The person asks themselves if they want to dive off the diving board. Perhaps they have seen that it is fun, and others have said it is fun too, or maybe they just instinctually know the rush would be enjoyable. They climb up the board and get ready.

2. They are then confronted with the real and present fear of the diving board. The sheer, frightening height of it, the distance to the water below. The mental heavy lifting required to overcome the fear becomes unbearable.

.

3. The mind makes a decision. It doesn't want to go back down the ladder. Going back down the ladder would be to admit defeat, and that also would be unbearable.

4. So the mind, in its infinite wisdom, makes a compromise. It decides that the safest place to be is the point of indecision. It gets the benefit of the thrill of pondering the jump, but without all the risk associated with actually jumping.

Now apply this same concept to the idea of having a problem:

1. The person asks themselves if they have a problem. They see all the evidence of the problem, maybe get some feedback, or just instinctively know there's a problem.

2. They are then confronted with the reality of how hard change actually will be: The habitual patterns of failure in trying to change, the disruption it will cause, and how uncomfortable the change will actually be. The mental heavy lifting required to overcome change becomes unthinkable.

3. The mind makes a decision. It doesn't want to completely go back to the old behavior because to

do so would be to admit defeat, which would be unbearable.

4. So the mind compromises by deciding that the safest place to be is at the point of indecision. Fantasy lives here. Wishing lives here. Perhaps small 'victories' do, too, such as getting into an argument with the loved one we have been duck-feeding, or some sarcastic comment or sideways glance. This gives us part of the thrill, but without the risk of actual change.

Do you see now, how, when confronted with pain, the human mind very powerfully activates its defenses in order to keep us 'safe'? And do you see how sinister this can be, keeping us stuck in the seemingly better option of small doses of pain over a long period of time, rather than one large pain?

As counselors, this makes it especially difficult to confront ambivalence. One has to honor the fact that it's not our place to break down your walls of defensiveness (because after all, they are there for good reason), yet simultaneously understand that this person is stuck precisely due to their lack of action.

So, once more, do I believe that everyone reading this

book is in denial? Of course not. But do I believe that you and I, as humans have difficulty seeing what is right in front of our faces, sometimes? Absolutely. More than likely, the act of asking that question is probably some sort of stalling technique to keep you stuck in ambivalence.

To help forward movement, I've compiled a list of some of the characteristics that may aid in solidifying precisely what the problem might be. This list came from thoughtful self-reflection, as well as feedback from clients, friends and colleagues. Take your time to honestly ask yourself if any of these concepts resound with you.

If you find yourself arguing with any of them on their merit (i.e., 'is this *really* a bad quality to have?'), consider whether the statement "I suffer a great deal because of this, and I could benefit from changing" is applicable.

Also consider whether or not you are arguing the point because your brain is actively working against change in order to keep you in comfortable ambivalence. I encourage you to sink into the idea of being aware of your own suffering; a suffering you may, through habit or compromise, may not even be aware of anymore.

1. When praised for my selflessness, I am outwardly modest, but internally I gain a deep sense of identity and nourishment from it.
2. I find myself drawn to "project ducks:" People or situations to whom/which I can provide emotional support.

3. With those "project ducks," I show a pattern of giving much more emotionally to the relationship, then becoming upset when they're emotionally unavailable for me when I need them.

4. I struggle with perfectionism. I need to have things I do be within my idea of perfection. If it's not perfect, I am often afraid other people may judge me as less than adequate.

5. My sense of self-worth is heavily tied to my accomplishments.

6. I have compassion and tolerance for everyone else's mistakes, but I don't allow myself that same luxury.

7. I stay loyal to people, even if they aren't loyal to me.

8. I instinctively feel compelled to help others solve their problems. I find myself offering unwanted advice, giving rapid-fire suggestions, or attempting to fix or save someone from their unwanted feelings.

9. I don't like discord, so when people get into arguments, I often find myself being the peacemaker.

10. I think a little bit of manipulation is worth it if the person ends up better off because of it.

11. When people mention that I'm a hard worker, almost to a fault, I wear that feedback like a badge of honor.

12. When I give until it hurts, I feel morally and spiritually better than others, because they aren't willing to sacrifice like I am.

13. I feel panicky when I don't know my role in a situation.
14. I feel uneasy unless I am working to make myself better. I have difficulty accepting myself for who I am.
15. I often find myself becoming upset that others are not putting as much into tasks or projects as I am, or often find myself feeling that the burden of completing a task falls onto my shoulders.
16. I feel guilty when I have to miss work or social events. I secretly feel that the world will fall apart without me there to hold it up.
17. I find myself focusing on other people's lives or problems as a way of keeping people out of mine.
18. I enjoy giving out advice, but become upset or defensive when I am confronted with my own behavior.
19. I am overly conscious of the way I come off to other people.
20. I've been told that I do too much for others.
21. The plight of the helpless affects me deeply, and I feel personally guilty or responsible if I don't give all I can.
22. I find myself apologizing often.
23. When I become aware of how often I apologize, I apologize for that too!

24. I am often hyper-aware of the feelings of others, and feel compelled to help people, even if they haven't asked for it.
25. As I read this list, a significant number of the items applied to me, and now I feel guilty.

There's no simple threshold for whether or not one has a problem with unhealthy helping, and it's certainly not contingent on how many items you could check on this list as to whether a person 'qualifies' for a label.

This is about your quality of life. Take a look at whether your behaviors, either knowingly or subconsciously, are in the way of you achieving a better quality of life and having less suffering.

I'm not suggesting that you should immediately try to cease the behaviors outlined in this checklist. The goal of the strategies and beliefs this book puts forth have to do with your quality of life.

There are many shades of gray when it comes to behavior. You may very well end up continuing these behaviors, but perhaps slightly tweaking your intentions and actions.

When that happens (for, even when you do the work, it will be *when* that happens and not *if*,) don't lose heart. This book also outlines strategies for returning to that area of self-exploration and the isolation of opportunities for growth within what looks like a crisis.

What's more, there is no universal template for Good

or Bad Behavior. It all depends on the individual. Sometimes, fowl pun intended, what's good for the goose may not be good for the gander.

But Isn't Compassion A Good Thing?

I get the inevitable pushback about this topic nearly every time I discuss it. Specifically, there are those that believe I am calling into question the nature of human interaction. Here is that loyal opposition's least-favorite phrase in response: "Yes, but:"

I really would prefer to scream and shout YES! I love compassion. I love compassionate people, and I love to share the joy of helping and being helped. Compassion is the cornerstone of our humanity. It's the force that drives all of us to connect, to get those good feelings of sharing with others. Compassion is the foundation for what brings us together, through our capacity to love.

My guess is that since you are reading this book, you probably have no shortage of compassion. So I imagine that I don't need to belabor the point. You have probably experienced the positive outcomes of compassion firsthand.

It actually makes us happier, and wiser. Those rating higher in the domain of compassion are actually physically healthier, show a reduced risk of various health problems, and get along better with others. As well, people that practice willful compassionate acts on a regular basis report better moods more often.

The good, healthy work that helpers do is never part of a problem. I would not have become a counselor if I didn't believe that helping others was worthwhile. Now the 'but': I won't suggest that compassion is a bad thing. However, unhealthy helping, like any number of behaviors, can be a good thing gone horribly wrong.

Compassion comes to us from the medieval Italian root-word *passo*, or suffering. Like many words in medieval Italian, the subtler meaning is lost by literal translation. Compassion does not merely mean to suffer with someone, or alongside them, but to share their burden, to work as a team in the way that we all do in healthy relationships. Pain shared is pain halved, as the old expression goes. But not pain perpetuated.

Compassion, the desire to help one another, is good. It is healthy and it is hard-wired into us. It is an integral piece of what makes up the human. To love and be loved, to help and be helped, are normal parts of our makeup, as hard-wired to us as our hands or our feet, and integral to our basic humanity.

Everyone cuts a finger at some point, stubs a toe or otherwise injures a hardwired extremity through normal wear and tear. Compassion can go similarly wrong.

When a normal processes of human functioning— eating, for example (the celebration of life through sustenance)—goes awry through compulsive eating, or compulsive restriction of food, this can have extremely harmful consequences.

Another example would be nervousness. This normal human feeling. which warns us of danger and invigorates us to take action can cause crippling dysfunction if left unchecked. Similarly, unhealthy helping is a sickness of compassion. It occurs when good intentions and kindness go wrong, whether it is because we aren't acting out of selflessness, we have an unhealthy compulsion that we can't stop doing, or because we simply don't know any better.

Acts of compassion are nourishing and beneficial to society, but when taken to an unhealthy extreme, the emotional energy behind codependence can be the culprit in a great deal of interpersonal conflict and suffering.

You might be asking, "Well, how do I know when compassion is a good thing and when it isn't?" While on a flight about a year ago, I had one of those proverbial 'A-ha!' moments that guided my answer to this question:

The flight attendants were presenting their in-flight emergency instructions. "And, remember," one flight attendant said, "If you're traveling with a child or someone who requires assistance, secure your own mask first, then assist the other person."

I'd heard this spiel dozens of times, but just accepted it. Curious, I asked an attendant about it, and got a very candid answer:

"In a midair cabin depressurization situation, you only have a few moments of oxygen before you pass out. To be frank, a child might not get to their mask in time and start to pass out. If a parent panics in this situation, and tries to help their child before themselves, the parent will likely pass out before their child and then both people will be in big trouble. It's better to secure your mask first, even if you have to run the risk of your loved one temporarily passing out. They will regain consciousness soon after you put their mask on."

A-ha! I was starting to understand why compassion can go so awry. We as human beings have a hardwired compunction to help each other. We get good feelings from this. It serves our needs as a community, and it's spiritually nourishing. But in this advanced, busy, complicated world we live in, it's hard to distinguish good helping from unhealthy helping.

Early humans never had to worry about whether bailing their child out of jail for the third time was a good idea or not. They never had to worry about how much money they should donate to a charitable organization, or for that matter what to do if that damned oxygen mask came down over their faces all of a sudden.

I asked a friend to imagine that she and her children were on an airplane with the cabin quickly depressurizing. She told me, "As a mother of three children, I get it. I know what I'm supposed to do, but, still, I would have a hard time doing it if I saw my babies in pain!"

Of course, you won't always be presented with the opportunity to stop and slow down to think about every little decision you make. What's more, our natural instinct to help others isn't necessarily bad, so I don't presume to ask anyone to suppress their desires.

What I'm suggesting is that we look at patterns in our behavior, use our natural instincts to guide us, and temper our decisions with wisdom. To do this, it becomes necessary to slow down, do a little bit of self-analysis, and ask ourselves some very important questions.

Back in Chapter 2, I asked the reader to use the metaphor of Not Feeding The Ducks as a metaphoric tool to help characterize the problem many of us face. Now I ask you to similarly apply the parable of the oxygen mask to life, and see if it may help guide your decisions when we ask some crucial questions.

Again, compassion is a wonderful thing. Hopefully, through reading this book and doing your own work on adjusting yourself, you will more fully comprehend true compassion. Before then however, ask yourself questions such as these:

- Are there unforeseen factors that haven't been considered?
- Is my "helpful" action actually hurting me?
- Will it, in the long run, hurt the person I am trying to help?
- Is my help even necessary, or wanted?
- Is what I am doing actually not true compassion, but a selfish compulsion?

- Do I need to put on my own oxygen mask of self-compassion first before helping others, so that I don't get burned out?

These are some very important concepts to consider. It will be up to you in the end to decide what fits best with your life. If you desire all the benefits of compassionate acts, it becomes necessary to cultivate the true willingness to take a more nuanced approach to self-reflection.

The more careful and deft this study is, the more the habits stick. Thus, the more Compassion finds us.

How It Happens

We know now that compassion can go wrong. To overcome this error, it's important to understand from a behavioral perspective how it is happening. I intend to make looking at your own behavior a very prosaic, scientific endeavor because, simply, that's what works.

I want you to take the same dispassionate, objective approach to this problem that you would take to a similarly objective subject such as mathematics.

Objectivity can be a real gift. How many times have you heard a friend or colleague describe a problem, only to see that because they are so wrapped up in the passion of their emotions, they can't see the solution right in front of them? When this happens to you take the approach that your problem is a problem, one with clear input and a clear solution.

Avoid the feedback loops of gossip, re-living your rage, fear or helplessness. Understand that people spend sometimes years in those feedback loops. A new paradigm is that your problem happened because of clear-cut reasons, and that there is also a clear-cut solution.

Again, I'm not removing the humanity from the problem, but focusing for a moment on solutions. Just like the aforementioned example of the brownie, just because I know what goes into a brownie doesn't make it any less delicious. Just because I am intentionally removing the emotion (both positive and negative) doesn't mean I can't come back to it. But if I'm trying to focus on, for example, why my brownies never seem to rise properly, rationality really needs to play a key role. During the non-artistic part of baking, I need to take away the epic narrative, and remember that a brownie is just flour, water, sugar, chocolate and similar basic ingredients.

Likewise, things that happen, when stripped of epic narrative, are just real-world events. William Shakespeare, who knew a lot about psychology for his day, said that "There's nothing good or bad but thinking makes it so."

While this sounds simple, putting it into practice is anything but easy at first. Even those who have a remarkable, sparkling self-awareness of their own problems that they can put into words well and address directly and emphatically in session… find that actually getting to the point where the brain goes haywire and employing the tools I give them in the manner we've been discussing is a hard, scary thing to do in practical fact.

It doesn't have to be. With practice, such recognition can become second nature. Emotional connection can come later. To be frank, much of this problem is likely because too much emotion is caught up in the relationship or experience.

An excellent example occurs in the Wachowski Brothers' 1994 film "The Matrix." The movie's hero Neo, a hapless wage-slave, discovers that the whole world around him is a computer mock-up, and that he has been plugged into the machine for his whole life. Throughout the movie, Neo has trouble truly believing that he is *actually* plugged into a computer, and has difficulty believing, in turn, that he can change the world around him simply by thinking that change into existence. Only when he's at the apex of his peril does Neo start to see the world for what it is, which is a screen of green zeros and ones, the binary code for the computer program.

Then he can finally manipulate the world around him, when he has mastered his own true understanding of it and not someone else's.

It is likewise important that we lay a groundwork of knowledge, so that you are seeing all the green zeroes and ones in your life; that is, the larger patterns behind everything you do, why you do it, and how to improve.

Reward Systems

I believe the best way to present this material to you is to avoid a lengthy treatise on the psychology of conditioning. Instead, let's focus on the very specific patterns that are happening when compassion goes wrong. There are four kinds of behavioral concepts at play when we talk about a broken compassion system.

Just as it was in "The Matrix", these are the inner workings of the little green zeroes and ones that make up your brain and your mind. They are reinforcement (positive and negative) and punishment (positive and negative).

Reinforcement (positive)

Earlier, it was mentioned that helping others triggers a positive evolutionary response in the brain. We'll call this a psychological reward. Behaviorists call this positive reinforcement.

It's your own little brain-treat; specifically a chemical called dopamine that you get when you do something that your brain associates with pleasure. So, I do X, and X gives me something good, and my brain responds, 'Yay, here's a reward!'

This is the most basic of all reward systems. Eventually the brain begins to expect, even anticipate, the reward. This helps the brain weed out any behaviors that aren't good for your survival.

Here are some basic examples:

- Being rewarded after a long work week with praise and acknowledgement and a pizza party.
- A gesture of appreciation from a friend after helping them move.
- Someone at your job shaking your hand and telling you, "Thank you for your service."
- A trusted advisor higher up in your field listening to your struggles and telling you you're doing Okay.
- Throwing some bread at ducks and smiling as you feel satisfaction from helping out.

Note that the term positive doesn't mean good, not outright. Similar meaning, but not exactly the same in this case. It simply means that whomever receives the reinforcement associates the behavior with the reward. For example, an underling at work who is praised for always having the coffee ready and the day's reports out is going to repeat the behavior because, in several ways, it makes their own job less stressful.

Punishment (positive)

Positive punishment also comes to us from operant conditioning. The terms 'positive' and 'punishment' may sound strange together. But what it is simply referring to is when a stimulus is added (hence the term positive) to a behavior.

This is also sometimes called punishment by application. Positive punishments are unpleasant stimuli meant to decrease a certain behavior. All of these are prime examples of positive punishment:

- A high school student getting disciplined for smoking in the Boy's Room.
- A drunk driver given a field sobriety test and a DUII.
- A child receiving a spanking for not going to bed on time.
- A cat biting you after you stroke it's fur the wrong way.

Punishment (negative)

Likewise, negative punishment involves taking away something that the subject likes if they either perform a wrong behavior or fail to perform a right one. This is also sometimes called punishment by removal.

Any fan of classic rock could probably cite the line from Pink Floyd's 'The Wall' immediately, wherein the schoolmaster yells, 'How can you have any pudding if you don't eat your meat?" An equally classic example from our own day involves any child getting their XBox privileges taken away for not doing a chore, or getting a bad grade.

When I was growing up, the good thing taken away in such instances was that I wasn't allowed to go play outside. This is the same idea: that a behavior causes a loss of something that the person views as desirable.

Reinforcement (negative)

There's a second reward system as well, one that works similarly to positive reinforcement but with a small twist. It's called negative reinforcement

Say you have a fear or anxious response to something. That fear is used to avoid behaviors or things that might invoke that fear response. Verbalized, this might sound like, "If I don't [x], The Bad Thing won't happen."

Thus, the subject eventually learns not to do [x] or to avoid it altogether. The actual reward comes with the thought or feeling that you have done something to narrowly escape something that would have been bad for you.

So your brain gives you that feeling of relief and accomplishment. Think of this part of your mind as your inner James Bond, receiving praise and adulation for saving the world from certain destruction yet again.

- Leaving early to get to work to avoid traffic.
- Waiting a half hour after eating before swimming.
- Calling in sick for your spouse when they are too hung over.

While all of these systems are at play in some form or another in life, I save this for last because this type of reinforcement is often the most pernicious in unhealthy helping, and in compassion gone haywire.

It seems that the most powerful reward systems are the ones associated with doing things to avoid a perceived catastrophe.

Specifically, with unhealthy helping it's often our fear of fear that actually drives this process. In other words, our fear of feelings we don't want to have. We're sure in our own minds that these emotions will hurt, so we avoid them.

Can you see, then, how often in your own life you may be exhibiting negative reinforcement in response to a problem? This process often occurs at times when we think we're being helpful but really just doing something to avoid fear, or overdose on the dopamine rush our brains produce from believing it has successfully avoided a catastrophe.

How often have you done something because of the thought of future negative emotions (fear, discomfort, awkwardness, shame, etc.) compelled you to act in a helpful manner in order to avoid them?

Reward Schedules

In addition to the kinds of rewards your brain can receive, there are also different schedules for those rewards. Systems of rewards concern 'what kind' of reward; while schedules concern 'how often' the reward occurs.

These are broken down into two sub-types, continuous reinforcement and partial reinforcement.

1. Continuous reinforcement

In this type of reinforcement, the behavior being rewarded is rewarded or reinforced every single time it happens. Every time I put a penny in a gumball machine, it gives me a gumball. Each time I raise my hand, the teacher calls on me.

2. Partial reinforcement

With partial reinforcement, the behavior is only reinforced part of the time, and dependent on a ratio or variable schedule.

Fixed-ratio schedule: This schedule involves reinforcement after a number of times performing an activity. Press a button five times, win a prize. Every fifth time wins one prize.

Variable-ratio schedule: This involves reinforcement after performing an activity an unpredictable number of times. A good example would be the randomness of fishing. Sometimes I throw the lure out ten times and get a fish. Sometimes I toss it out twice and get one. Sometimes I toss it out thirty times and get a fish, etc.

Fixed-interval schedule: Similar to the fixed-ratio schedule, but this has to do with the amount of time that passes between rewards. A classic example of a fixed-ratio schedule would be getting a paycheck after seven days of work. 7 days = 1 paycheck.

Variable-interval schedule: Again, very similar to the variable-ratio schedule in that there is no predictability to the amount of time that passes before a reward is given. Sometimes I wait three days and get friend's text back. Sometimes one day. Sometimes a month, etc.

Similar to negative reinforcement, with unhealthy helping a variable-interval or variable ratio schedule is the most prevalent. This is because, as humans, we tend to stick around the longest when we can't predict when and how we are going to get a reward.

This seems to be amplified with rewards we really, really want, as well. Ask any casino manager which schedule is the best, and they'll tell you every time that a variable-ratio, variable interval reward schedule will keep old Bessy blue-hair at her gamblin' chair the longest. We get stuck constantly putting quarters in various metaphoric slot machines in our lives trying to get our reward from it.

The Lazy Brain

In addition to rewards and schedules, the brain is also working with the concept I call the 'lazy brain'. The brain, for all of its infinite marvels and wondrous complexities, is a machine that desires simplicity.

The brain has evolved over time to essentially determine how to get the most out of spending the least amount of energy. Without getting into a lengthy discussion about neurobiology, for the sake of a working understanding we'll call this the brain's desire to achieve the path of least resistance.

To the brain, good enough is…well, good enough. Consider two cases, and the parallels between them. There are many other factors at play with both of these examples, but for the sake of understanding I've simplified them:

Let's say you are procrastinating on a project, in this instance studying for an exam. The brain is now confronted with a problem, and does some very complex yet simple math.

So, in the case of the procrastinator, the individual is sitting around, lazily eating potato chips while watching TV.

Perhaps dread, fear, anxiety or worry about needing to finish the project comes up. The brain does not like this one bit. Conventional wisdom would think that the brain would do the hard work to gird up the loins, buckle down and get into that homework.

But we know this is often not the case, right? That's because the brain is trying to be the smart miser that it is, and save that energy for something in the future that might be deemed more important.

A part of your brain brought up an inconsistency: The fact that you see yourself as a studious person, the fact that the homework is due, and the fact that you need time to complete it. But, to the brain, those are also painful realities, and ones that demand a great deal of attention and psychic resources.

So, instead of doing the hard, painful work that it would take to confront the emotionally draining reality that you have been procrastinating, it instead will develop a compromise. The brain will simply divert attention elsewhere.

Or maybe, the brain will agree that it's an acceptable alternative to open your book while watching TV. It'll sink in through osmosis, right? Or maybe you will convince yourself that you can watch another hour of TV and study later. The brain says, 'Good one, brain. Nice thinking,' and it's back to munching chips and flipping through channels. Voila! Good enough is good enough.

Or, consider a spouse who is thinking about getting out of an abusive relationship. Let's apply that same logic. As the person is thinking about it, some very painful, very difficult truths are going to come up, truths which the brain probably can't handle. This is where we see the brain spring into action and activate all those wondrous defense mechanisms we see (projection, deflection, etc.).

The path of least resistance demands that the brain not spend the tremendous energy drain confronting all the defenses we put up. That's hard work. A simpler solution has to be easier, right? So the brain makes the decision to perhaps try again in the relationship. It's comfortable, it's predictable, it's good enough.

You have actually rewarded the brain for being lazy! Classic negative reinforcement. The brain had a fear, and it enacted a behavior that made that fear go away. In turn, the brain thinks this is good, because you were in a high-anxiety state.

Then something you did; to ignore, change the subject, become defensive, project, deflect, etc., made the extreme negative feeling go away. It replaced an extreme negative feeling with an unsatisfactory, yet ultimately more comfortable feeling.

Good enough is good enough. This leaves you solving the immediate problem (how to not feel intense negative emotions), but in the long term spiritually unfulfilled.

Putting it all together

These three behavioral concepts seem to be common themes that I have seen explain much of what is going on behind the scenes of unhealthy helping. At times they all work together to become a form of mental trap that is often difficult for us to escape. Essentially, you're at the mercy of some type of reward schedule that is compelling you to continue the behavior in an attempt to create a solution to a problem.

Here's another example. Let's try to spot what all is going on here. As mentioned, this is a thoroughly simplified version of what is happening inside the brain, just to accentuate the point.

Let's say you're trying to train a dog to stop scratching the door to come in. Prior to this, every time the dog scratched the door, you let him in (continuous positive reinforcement). Now suddenly, you stop opening the door when the dog scratches. Gah! It's getting worse. By switching the schedule of reinforcement to a variable ratio, you're training the dog to actually do the behavior more. In doing so, it will actually take longer for the dog to get the hint to stop scratching.

The dog scratches. If you let that dog in, after it scratches a few times, whines, barks, scratches again, and whines a few times, you have just created the most sinister reward system for this poor pup.

You've now taught it that if it wants to get what it wants, it needs to sit down at the slot machine o' rewards, and start plugging quarters in until it randomly gets what it wants, with no fixed schedule or ratio.

And you've actually just conditioned yourself in a very similar manner. You've just rewarded yourself for avoiding the negative feeling of guilt or shame, by giving the dog what it wants. You perhaps added a little bit of embarrassment or frustration, but again, the lazy brain prefers 'minor embarrassment' to 'major guilt.'

Yet rewarding yourself for avoiding something, in the end, takes far more work and far higher of a personal toll than the minimal effort it would take to train the dog away from the behavior. This apparent conundrum perfectly illustrates the difference between knowing the full scope of something and actually carrying out whatever it takes to truly and honestly change how we see and react.

Our misapplied compassion says that we shouldn't be so mean to the poor, amoral, defenseless four-legged child, begins minimizing the actual true effect of the problem, and skews off on any number of epic narratives that don't apply to actually training the dog away from the behavior.

Positive reinforcement would involve, in its simplest sense, rewarding the correct behavior in the animal, for at least the minimum number of times necessary for the dog to associate the correct behavior or series of behaviors with the reward. That reward can be changed or variegated, and altered in frequency depending on what you're trying to train the dog to do, the necessity for and scope of correction or redirection in the behavior itself, and what you want the dog to learn.

Likewise, positive punishment would be any sort of punishment that the animal was taught to associate as a natural consequence of negative behavior.

Negative reinforcement, similar in approach, would involve the animal getting an endorphin-reward from escaping some cue when it began to slip back into the old behavior (as humans can likewise self-recognize when backsliding, which will be discussed in later chapters.)

The problem with negative reinforcement in humans and animals alike is that without the positive, we are merely living in fear of some behavior, without a sufficient counterattraction.

The fear of fear colors our perceptions until we are as twitchy as an animal that has been trained violently or cruelly. It's not enough, in a symbolic sense, to avoid the dark from fear; but also to reach for the light in hope. In a continuously-reinforced reward schedule, the dog would be rewarded every time it performed the correct behavior or series of behaviors.

It is up to the preference of their human, of course, but over time this would become impractical overkill in most cases, and unhealthy in that the animal is no longer challenged to learn or behave correctly without needing an external reward.

A good example of a partially-reinforced reward schedule would be, from the dog's perspective, "Hey, if I only go to the bathroom indoors on those newspapers long enough, Mama will start letting me back in the living room more and more, and perhaps eventually take down the doggy-gate."

71

A partially-reinforced reward schedule at a variable ratio is one that most people with dogs end up falling back on: that the animal knows if it behaves well, sooner or later in the course of every normal day there will be acknowledgement in some form or another. This is that animal's own path of least resistance toward wanting to live in a pack with you the human, for the benefits that both derive.

A fixed-interval reward schedule would involve the animal being shown that if there were weeks when any sort of negative behavior did not show up, that meant a ride in the car and a Big Walk off the leash someplace in the woods.

Dogs learn this particular schedule well, I have found. A variable-interval reward schedule would be one which reinforces, in the dog's mind, the precept that, "If I keep acting this way, my human will keep doing things of that nature."

The dog wants to do the minimum amount necessary to keep living in a friendly pack with you, and no more. Your own path of least resistance is similar: Whatever it takes to keep the dog as low-maintenance as possible.

In between, we find that they are our children, and we must not warp them if we want them to act right. In the long run, hiding from training the animal is tantamount to hiding from our own intense feelings rather than using them to grow.

In both cases, the adage that an old dog can't be taught new tricks is a cop-out. With enough follow-through, any behavior can be re-learned, or unlearned.

And Moving On

"The curious paradox is that when I accept myself just as I am, then I can change"

CARL R. ROGERS, On Becoming a Person 1961

I n my experience, inevitably after the 'How it Happens' conversation, the mind's tendency is to move into the 'But Why?'

An important question to be sure. For each individual, the answer to why will be slightly different, but otherwise fundamentally the same. And, we will come to learn as well that more important than dwelling on it, is to properly grieve the why.

We are psychologically wounded when we are blindsided by something traumatic that happens to us. It can affect our sense of control, our sense of trust, our fear of abandonment, grief, and dependence just to name a few.

These wounds can have neural or physiological effects endemic to any bad fright or jarring change. And this plays out in our lives in fascinating and sometimes abjectly frustrating ways. Often this creates a particularly gnarly and sinister feedback loop that we stay stuck in for months, even years at a time.

We stay in these loops for any number of reasons. When it comes to relationships, for example, we imagine that we are making allowances or changing ourselves in order to earn this partnership we Have To Have. In the 1996 Cameron Crowe movie "Jerry MacGuire," the main character (played by Tom Cruise), uttered the now famous line from the movie, "You...complete me."

Romantic, to be sure, and perhaps for many, a wonderful expression of the healthy symbiosis that goes into sharing a life with another. I have often however within the confines of unhealthy relationships found this to be a problematic concept altogether.

In my work as a couples counselor, I have come across no greater problem than the concept that your partner is supposed to somehow complete you. In fact, I would feel confident to say that this is often the primary and only problem that is presented in problematic couples work.

Joe's Story

Joe described himself as a giver. For all his dating life he was, as many of us are, looking for his true love. In his search, he often lavished his girlfriends with attention, gifts, and time.

Yet somehow, Joe could never find a relationship that worked. He often found himself in the unfortunate and frustrating position of being quite needy for reciprocation of time and attention from his girlfriends, and would often express frustration, resentment and eventually break up due to what he felt was a lack of mutuality and support in the relationship. Joe also described himself as a bit of a doormat.

Joe's relationship with his mother had never been good. She was a classic alcoholic. She raised him as a single mother, and essentially when she wasn't working, she was drinking. He grew up as what some would call a 'latch-key' kid, and raised himself. Joe recalls for most of his life always having a nagging fear of abandonment.

In my office, Joe finally began to understood that for his whole dating life he'd been looking for the relationship that he never had with his mother. Until he could give himself what he desperately wanted others to give him, he would never truly be happy. He was having a wonderful epiphany.

Joe began lamenting on how all of his relationships had this common thread. He would meet a woman, court her, and shower her with love and adulation. In return, his hopes were that he could pour all of his sense of identity into them, all of his love, trust, hope and self.

Inevitably, he was woefully let down (as anyone would be, because what he proposed was quite impossible) and was then disappointed in his relationships. He often attracted women as equally unavailable (both in terms of time commitments and emotional ones).

With his romantic recreations of his childhood psychodrama, Joe so much wanted, and needed from these women what his mother was unable to give him, which was to be there for him as a young child. Because of this, he was left with a sense of abandonment, forced to recreate and live out his lack of fulfillment again and again through adult romantic relationships. He deeply hoped that one relationship, the love of an intimate partner, could give him that sense of satisfaction that he never had. Unfortunately for him and his potential mates, they could never give him what he needed. Joe needed an internal sense of acceptance, something that sometimes children never have the opportunity to learn and acquire.

The fact of the matter is that for Joe, no woman or relationship would ever be enough to fulfill that need. It's simply unrealistic for Joe to expect any person to give him an internal sense of identity and support.

And for many of us, what is the odd paradox for Joes is that even though he was now trapped by his own fixation on the desire to have another person give him what he now could easily give himself. It wasn't until Joe came to this realization, and was able to properly grieve loss of acceptance and love that every child needs, that he was able to give this to himself, and move on.

This is the paradox, or Chinese finger trap that many of us get stuck in so often. We desperately seek validation and support from others. when with a little bit of emotional re-tooling and hard work, we could give to ourselves. But we don't want to give it to ourselves, because we're so mad, sad or frustrated that it wasn't given to us that we get stuck trying to make a non-workable strategy work.

Very often, we find ourselves smack-dab in the middle of that paradox, hopelessly spinning on a hamster wheel going nowhere. While I certainly am not suggesting that all of us that struggle with issues of this nature, we owe it to ourselves to delve into our motivations for why we choose to be so helpful, to be so compassionate, to see what lies underneath.

Tim's Soup

Many years ago I had an 'a-ha' moment that accentuated this paradox, and how pervasive and integrated this problem of unhealthy helping was in my life.

While at work, I was in the lunchroom enjoying a bowl of soup. If you are anything like me, when you get into a good bowl of soup there's a great deal of sipping, slurping, smiling and deep grunts of approval.

About halfway through the bowl, a colleague and friend of mine, Tim, came into the break room. Being a practiced observer of human behavior, plus knowing a bit about my friend, I could tell that Tim was not in a good mood. My old inner voice of discomfort started to enter in.

I started to feel that nagging tightness in my chest, that voice of fear and panic. The idea that because someone around me wasn't okay, that I wasn't safe. He came in and hurriedly slumped down into a chair, nodding to me in his presence. He had a furled brow and appeared preoccupied. We sat in silence for a few moments.

As we discussed in the chapter I thought I would "make' Tim feel better by somehow making myself smaller to him. I also knew that if I 'made' Tim feel better, I in turn would feel better.

"Tim I want to apologize if I am slurping my soup too loud. It's really good and I'm enjoying it."

One of the reasons that Tim is my friend is because he is known in his personal and professional life for his brutal honesty. He knows me and what I struggle with, and knew this would be an excellent opportunity for a teaching moment. He's also a very funny guy.

"John," Tim said with a playful grin, "Understand one thing. I'm a recovering addict. People like me, we're not like you. You're worried about how your soup sounds; I'm sitting here trying to figure out how to get *your soup* into *my stomach.*"

We smiled and had a laugh about the whole thing. But Tim also very cleverly gave me a valuable and necessary insight into the world. It was the crushing reality that my feelings at that particular moment weren't even on his radar.

I had no clue what was going on for Tim at that moment. Sitting in silence, my inability to tolerate the discomfort of knowing why a friend was in pain, I made all sorts of assumptions. I assumed it was about me.

What did I do wrong? What if he hates me forever? If I did something wrong, I better fix it, or something bad might happen. I never even questioned whether or not he wanted or even needed my help. I just assumed he did.

I discovered about myself that day the idea that for most of my life I operated under the assumption that *the safest place for me emotionally, was inside your head.*

The problem of unhealthy helping, the dysfunctional pattern of beliefs and behaviors that I had adopted, kept me in a neurotic, fearful place where my sense of well-being and happiness were predicated on whether the world accepted me as a person or not.

I came to the realization that day of how much time and energy I actually spend on a daily basis doing this. I had developed entire schemas of belief about this. So much of my personality and identity had developed around this concept. It's probably no surprise that this was partially the reason I became a counselor!

But because of this paradox, because of past pain and my inability to move past it, I was looking for in others what I couldn't do. I was spilling my emotional junk out all over the place trying to get what I simply could have just given myself, which was the reassurance that I'm a good person, that I am okay, that I don't need to be inside Tim or anybody else's head, that I am safe, and that I deserve a voice of my own.

And that my pursuit of delicious soup isn't selfish, it isn't uncaring, and in fact, for my sake and for his, that level of self-involvement is actually the best place for me to be right in that moment.

I had done a tremendous amount of self-work before this happened, but this was a significant leap forward of insight. That day I resolved to stop the insanity, and start to take a harder look into how and why my brain does what it does. I resolved to become more aware of my thinking and feeling and how it leads to my behaviors. And each day, a little bit closer to my goals, with a lot of hard work and a little bit of luck, I have been doing better ever since.

So Now What?

"Yesterday I was clever, so I wanted to change the world.
Today I am wise, so I am changing myself."

RUMI (13th Century Poet)

I n my own pursuit of the truth, I've read hundreds of books and spent over two decades, analyzing, learning, exploring and re-examining trying to bring about some peace and resolution to my issues. So it would be idealistic and unreasonable to assume that this one book can solve any or all of your problems.

Ironically as well, being the self-appointed hero child in my family, often burdened with the impossible task of fixing an impossible situation with underwhelming resources (and actually having the irrational belief that I, SuperJohn could somehow do that), it would be me actually feeding my own ducks to assume so.

So, no, rather than presuming I can or need to show you how to climb Mount Everest, I have shown you first, why it's important to have some safety gear, and then given you directions to the store.

Much of the rest will be up to use what insights you have learned and will learn, from this book, other books, counseling, group discussions, conversation with friends, late night crying sessions, email to a boss, missed opportunity in life, breakup, makeup, conference, or any other source, to take with you on that wonderful journey.

As the author, I have to also give myself permission to say that I may have missed some things. The good news is there are plenty of other wonderful writers who also offer signposts of equal caliber.

In arriving at this point in our process, I want to reiterate that there is no magic bullet here, no situational panacea in paperback form that will Always Fix Everything. No one book can solve every single problem with a finite series of methods.

I can get you pointed in the right direction, but at its core this book is a work of psychological Philosophy, designed to agitate, ignite and inspire change.

Rather than a How-To manual for not feeding the ducks, this book seeks to list all the reasons Why this is a good thing not to do. (Perhaps the How-To manual could be a sequel, but something tells me it would be a lot more work, and no two results would be alike.)

With that all being said, it should be a little more apparent now why it's not possible to skip to the end of this book. The working aspect of full self-awareness comes at the end, not right out. If someone comes to me asking how they could change another person, in just those terms, this chapter would make no sense whatsoever without the insight and awareness contained in the previous.

You couldn't have read this chapter first and had it make any sense without first going through all parts of the process. More than a set of parlor tricks, these are tools to shore up hard work. No tool can do an actual job, merely facilitate it.

So Now What?

Unlearning the belief systems outlined in the previous chapters has to come first. When the brain goes haywire, your objectivity is compromised. You need a looking glass that is still and serene enough to reflect back all the parts of you that are still in the dark and blocking the light.

Seeking help, in whatever necessary form, is and will be the most important part of the journey. You can't do it alone, and no matter how heroic or messianic it might seem, you don't need to. But guess what? You will need to do more.

In order to begin to get out of our own way, the internal paradigm for how we see things must shift. We must challenge ourselves out of the safe, comfortable ruts we have built that inhibit true self-examination, growth and change.

One doesn't learn to ride a horse overnight. But the first and most challenging part is to get on said horse to begin with. This book isn't meant to solve all your problems by any stretch.

A good initial strategy is to question your chain of beliefs: What you believe, why you believe it, and how those beliefs determine your habits and actions. In order to make this work, you'll need to be aware of subtle beliefs that slip into your chain of logic.

It's important in the early stages of change that you assess and evaluate your progress. Too often, I've noted in that after I introduce these concepts to a client, they come back a week later telling me they didn't work.

It must be noted that for a while, like a child who picks up a basketball for the first time and begins to dribble, you are going to feel awkward and uncoordinated. Eventually, you will start to pick up some skill. No one can uncrate a violin and play the Bach Double Concerto. Practice makes perfect. First attempts rarely do.

Likewise, start with small, attainable victories. The aforementioned child should stick to dribbling and shooting. Trying to play against LeBron James two days after learning the game isn't going to work.

Similarly, start with simple boundaries that you can effectively hold. Trying to solve your long-standing 15 year dysfunctional marriage one week after learning these concepts probably isn't going to work. But perhaps learning how to say no to homeless people who ask you for money will.

A part of what makes emotional change effective is the belief that much of what you believe leads to less than stellar results. There is healing in the concept of saying, "Okay, clearly what I have been doing hasn't been working, so I'm willing to try something uncomfortable, something that I don't have faith in, to get some resolution to my problems."

Question your chain of beliefs. Before making decisions, before speaking, see what piece of logic or emotion compels you to say what you are saying or do what you are doing. Be bold in your willingness to pick apart the minutiae of your belief systems. Are you saying or doing something to invoke change in your life, or are your thoughts betraying your goals?

Whether conscious or subconscious, the belief that "I'm terrible at this. I will never be any good at this," self-reinforces frustration, failure and ill physical health. These ducks are internal... but they can be fed.

A Note on Mindfulness

"...the plan will happen in spite of us, not because of us."

MELODY BEATTIE

In keeping with the general thesis that this is a philosophy book and not a how-to manual, I won't give you treatise on mindfulness. There are many strategies and tools that one can employ any time there is dissonance. You will find what works best for you. But no matter what the situation, a still mind is almost always the first step that needs to be taken.

Sitting With It

Here we return to the previously-mentioned notion that when the brain goes haywire, there is a loss of one's objectivity in the moment. "Sit with it," psychologists, therapists and counselors often say. "Sit with the feeling."

No other instructions are used to follow this up, at first. It sounds deceptively simple. It's not. When attending a meditation-practice workshop many years ago, I was told by the instructor, "When you meditate, it's okay to have thoughts. Just don't follow them."

In meditation, we let our racing thoughts run their full course, like ripples on water, until that water eventually becomes still, or close enough to still to reflect unbroken light. So it is, in an even more basic sense than the most basic form of meditational practice, when we sit with our supposedly uncontrollable feelings.

These are the feelings we don't want to face, the ones we numb out with through any number of crutches that do not help us learn to walk through this kind of fire.

Saying 'No'

Sometimes, we are not allowed the luxury of time to sit with our feelings until they become manageable. Another strategy is to simply say No to those feelings, to not let them change our previous course of action, whereas beforehand they might have completely derailed it in whatever short or long-term sense.

Sometimes, saying no to feelings that change or hamstring our lives in ways we don't want is a matter of simply telling our brains to go sit in the corner while we finish what needs to get done.

A classic and powerfully allegorical example of Saying No occurs in another science-fiction movie, called "Cloud Atlas". Tom Hanks' primitive-tribesman character is confronted with many doubts, which manifest in the form of a humanoid Devil cursing and spouting filth and nonsense into his ear.

There is never a point where this character can be physically slaughtered. The only way this particular phantom can be defeated is to turn away from it and act as though it does not exist...or at the very least, to acknowledge everything those difficult feelings are telling you without giving in to what you thought they meant before.

Often, when we say no to such feelings, they drastically change form, and we find that their import was overestimated.

Breathing Through It

There are many parts to this strategy. The classic Annie Proulx short story "Brokeback Mountain" contains the equally classic line, "If you can't fix it, you gotta stand it." 'Standing it' in technical practice can be traced back as far as Stoic philosophers such as Epictetus, who advised in all things to consider "those things which are in your power, versus those which were never in your power and cannot be."

When sitting with a feeling, focusing and centering on one's own breath is the most basic meditational practice there ever was, requiring no special discipline or dogma. I have told many patients, "Breathe your way out, then think your way out." This, too, becomes an acquired skill through repetition.

Eventually, when we are reminded of a wounding, we can grieve it in the moment completely, using such techniques, rather than let it put scratches on the surface of the present moment.

When sitting with/breathing through something, a mantra, or simple affirming phrase, can be repeated to clear the mind of all external things. There is the Sanskrit "Om mani padme om" ('The jewel is in the lotus') that most people associate with the word mantra, but many more are everywhere. I used to use a three-line Primus St. John poem I saw posted on a public bus: "I believe in myself slowly. It takes all the doubt I have. It takes my wonder."

Breathing through it need not be passive. A good long walk, a hot shower, or any low-mental-stimulation but high-impact physical activity will also invoke the parasympathetic calming response in the brain, which shuts off the hysterical cascade of adrenalin and cortisol that comes when we drive ourselves into a panic attack about something.

When done mindfully, active or passive meditation techniques at the basic level eventually level off one's mood to a point where, eventually, we can ask, "Did I really get *that* upset about this particular thing?"

Other strategies abound, but most are variations on the three simple starter strategies listed above. In some way, you sit with it, you say no, you breathe through it…and then a new perspective comes. Please believe that it does. You're still reading, so I believe you do.

Conclusion

"So, does that make sense?"

Every time I catch myself almost asking a client that, or anyone in conversation, I have to smile. One of my earliest clinical supervisors used to call that to my attention frequently. It implies that I need validation for what I say because there is some doubt somewhere.

Even at this later phase of my own long journey, I catch myself doing that, and correct for it.'

But did this make sense? (Author removes tongue from cheek so reader knows to laugh).

Goodbyes are hard for me. I'm sure that you the reader can identify with this. I hold onto the irrational fear that I am somehow responsible for your success. That particular duck gets no more food past this page.

No matter how hard it is for me to say goodbye, the healthy route is to trust in the wisdom and intelligence of the reader, and to know when to let go. Ducks know when to build their nests, and when to find their food, and need none from me, only the coexistence and enjoyment of my company.

I've always tried to say goodbye in papers, books, and many other ways, the way Mr. Rogers did on the old children's program. I like to let the person down easy. I tell them what a good time I had with them, give them a courtesy recap of everything so that they can have a handy heuristic to take away from the experience (in the manner of a short synopsis or reminder of our intended purpose), and then end on some emotionally profound note.

Call it the counselor in me, or the codependent, I'm not sure which. But it satisfies my need for resolution of dissonance. We did what we could together. Now you get to go find your tribe. You get the motivation to keep going, the tension of being on the path. Even as a practiced practitioner, I have to recalibrate, relearn, and re-motivate.

Get help. Keep reworking it, and know you are worth it. Keep learning. Fall down. Skin both knees, get up, try again, laugh at yourself, have fun with it, cry, get serious, get angry, learn again, but DON'T GIVE UP, and above all, don't feed those damn ducks!

About the Author

John Raven, MS, CADC-II is a mental-health counselor, substance abuse professional, and long-time duck enthusiast. An explorer at heart, with roots from Wisconsin to Alaska, he has traveled much of the United States with an enthusiastic desire to share his insights and passion for wellness. A current resident of Portland, Oregon, he serves his clients through community courses, life coaching, and one-to-one counseling with individuals, couples and groups.